SCIENCE FILES

energy

OIL & GAS

Please visit our web site at: www.garethstevens.com
For a free color catalog describing Gareth Stevens Publishing's
list of high-quality books and multimedia programs,
call 1-800-542-2595 (USA) or 1-800-387-3178 (Canada).
Gareth Stevens Publishing's fax: (414) 332-3567.

Library of Congress Cataloging-in-Publication Data

Parker, Steve.
    Oil & gas / by Steve Parker.
      p. cm. — (Science files. Energy)
    Includes bibliographical references and index.
    ISBN 0-8368-4031-3 (lib. bdg.)
    Contents: Origins of oil and gas — Where in the world? — Oil and gas exploration — Big rigs —
Drilling deep — Rig to refinery — At the oil refinery — Fuels from oil — Natural gas — Plastics from
oil and gas — Raw materials — Powering the world — Oil and gas future?
    1. Petroleum—Juvenile literature. 2. Natural gas—Juvenile literature. [1. Petroleum. 2. Natural
gas.] I. Title.
    TN870.3.P37   2004
    665.5—dc22   2003060563

This North American edition first published in 2004 by
Gareth Stevens Publishing
A World Almanac Education Group Company
330 West Olive Street, Suite 100
Milwaukee, WI 53212 USA

Original edition © 2002 by David West Children's Books. First published in Great Britain
in 2002 by Heinemann Library, Halley Court, Jordan Hill, Oxford OX2 8EJ, a division
of Reed Educational and Professional Publishing Limited. This U.S. edition © 2004 by
Gareth Stevens, Inc. Additional end matter © 2004 by Gareth Stevens, Inc.

David West Editor: James Pickering
Picture Research: Carlotta Cooper
Gareth Stevens Editor: Carol Ryback
Gareth Stevens Designer: Kami Koenig
Cover Design: Melissa Valuch

Photo Credits:
Abbreviations: (t) top, (m) middle, (b) bottom, (l) left, (r) right

CORBIS: Front cover, 3, 4–5, 5(b), 5(mr), 7(bl), 9(bl), 10(bl), 10–11(t), 11(mr), 11(br), 12(tl), 12–13(t),
13(bl), 14(bl), 15(ml), 15(bl), 16(tr), 16(bl), 17(br), 18(bl), 18–19, 20–21(t), 20–21(b), 21(tl), 21(bl),
22(tm), 22(bl), 23(mr), 23(br), 25(tl), 25(mr), 26–27, 27(bl), 28–29(t), 29(br), 30(tr).
Still Pictures: Adrian Arbib 6(br); John Isaac 9(br); Thomas Raupach 18(br); Mark Edwards 24(bl);
Jorgen Schytte 26(br); Dylan Garcia 27(br); Pierre Gleizes 30(ml).
Katz/FSP: 8(bl), 12(br), 13(tr), 14(tr), 14(br), 15(mr), 17(tr), 25(bl), 27(tr), 30(bl).
Spectrum Colour Library: 12(bl).
Castrol: 20(bl), 21(mr).
Robert Harding Picture Library: S. Keep 21(tr).
Rex Features: 23(tr).
British Plastics Foundation: 25(bm).
Hitachi: 28–29(b), 29(tr).

Printed in the United States of America

1 2 3 4 5 6 7 8 9 08 07 06 05 04

OIL & GAS

Steve Parker

Gareth Stevens Publishing
A WORLD ALMANAC EDUCATION GROUP COMPANY

CONTENTS

4

INTRODUCTION

Oil — this dark, thick goo is one of the world's most vital sources of energy. We call it "petroleum," "crude oil," or "black gold," and process it into gasoline, diesel, and other fuels for cars, trucks, airplanes, furnaces, factories, and power plants. Natural gas forms under the same conditions as oil. Oil and gas products include plastics, paints, and countless other products. The oil and gas trade virtually controls our global economy.

Rig workers (left) connect sections of a drill "string" to bore deep into the earth and tap new oil supplies.

Oil refineries are massive industrial plants that split oil into its many constituents — separate parts (above).

Supertankers (left) transport enormous amounts of crude oil around the globe. Many weigh more than half a million tons (tonnes).

ORIGINS OF OIL AND GAS

Billions of years ago, long before dinosaurs roamed Earth, microscopic plants and animals lived, died, and slowly fell to the bottom of the prehistoric oceans in layers. Oil and natural gas formed from those tiny plants and animals.

Like water in a sponge, oil collects and moves through porous rock.

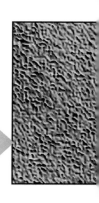

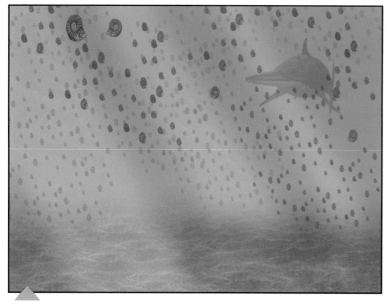

Ancient oceans swarmed with a "planktonic soup" — extremely tiny creatures and plants.

DEATHBED

A constant "rain" of trillions of minute phytoplankton (plants) and zooplankton (animals) in the prehistoric oceans died, sank, and were buried in layers of mud on the ocean floor. Under immense pressure and depth, they were squashed, heated, and partly rotted to form oil and gas.

HOW OIL AND GAS FORMED

Ooze on the ancient ocean floor slowly "pressure-cooked" under the weight and heat as more layers of trillions of tiny plants and animals piled up.

1 Tiny ocean organisms died and sank.

2 Layers built up under pressure and heat (about 176°–212° F; 80°–100° C).

In some areas, pools of oil and tar seep up to the surface. Most of these deposits were used up long ago.

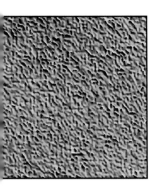

TRACED BACK TO THE SUN

Oil and gas are a form of stored solar energy that contain chemical energy in the links, or "bonds," between their tiny particles, or atoms. Animals in the ancient plankton got this energy by eating plants which grew in sunlight (just like plants today).

The dead matter partly decayed into a thick liquid (oil) and produced (natural) gas bubbles — both lighter than the water in the rock. The oil and gas seeped up through tiny holes, or pores, until a "trap" of nonporous (completely solid) rock stopped their upward movement. Earthquakes and water movement shifted the positions of the oil and gas.

3 Oil and gas formed and seeped upward under nonporous rock.

4 A salt dome split the oil and gas reservoir.

5 Earth movements cracked and folded the rock layers.

Gas

Oil

Water

An oil well in a cornfield

Green **ISSUES**

Oil and gas occur under many areas of the oceans and underground. Drilling for these resources often causes great environmental harm. While a flat farm field is only slightly disturbed by a well, wild areas and ocean beds are greatly changed by the rigs, pipelines, heavy machinery, and noises.

WHERE IN THE WORLD?

Oil and gas deposits occur in more than half of the countries around the world, but often in small and patchy amounts. The largest oil fields are in the Middle East; the largest natural gas fields are in Russia.

AROUND THE WORLD

The oil business began almost one hundred fifty years ago in eastern North America. It provided fuel for lamps and oil-burning heaters. In the 1890s, motor vehicle use increased, which boosted the need for gasoline. Huge oil fields were discovered in Texas and the Middle East in the 1930s, and in Alaska and Russia during the 1960s. Even more oil was discovered in Siberia (part of Russia) in the 1990s.

NORTH
AMERICA

SOUTH
AMERICA

■ Known supplies of oil and gas

□ Possible supplies of oil and gas

Known, or "proved," oil and gas fields exist in many parts of the world. New areas that may also hold oil and gas remain to be explored.

Oil companies are some of the richest companies in the world. Their main offices are often huge skyscrapers — such as the Petronas Towers in Kuala Lumpur, Malaysia.

Mountainous rocks known as "oil shale" hold "locked up" stores of oil in Colorado, Wyoming, and Utah. This type of oil is costly and difficult to extract.

RUSSIA

EUROPE

AFRICA

SOUTHEAST ASIA

MIDDLE
EAST

AUSTRALIA

OIL RESERVES TODAY

The Middle East has more than two-thirds of the world's known oil reserves. One nation, Saudi Arabia, has about one quarter of the total. Next come Central and South America, Africa, Russia, North America, Southeast Asia and Australia, and Europe. Oil is measured in barrels. Saudi Arabia has about 260,000 billion barrels. The U.S. has about 22,000 billion.

Green ISSUES

Oil is so valuable that nations often go to war over it. In 1990, Iraq invaded its tiny neighbor, Kuwait, and tried to capture its oil fields. During the Persian Gulf War that followed, many Kuwaiti oil fields were deliberately set on fire. Oil slicks caused immense environmental damage in the Persian Gulf.

Oil fields blaze during the Persian Gulf War in 1991.

OIL AND GAS EXPLORATION

Thousands of surveyors, geologists, and other experts constantly search — or prospect — for new oil and natural gas reserves using the latest electronics and technology.

IN THE AIR

Earth's surface gives scientists clues for where to look for underground oil and natural gas. Sometimes these areas are detected from high above — or even from outer space. The shape and color of the land, bare rock, and how the land or rock absorbs solar (the Sun's) heat help identify where to drill.

THE SEARCH FOR CLUES

Satellite images (1), aerial photographs (2), and radar (3) provide increasingly accurate surface maps for prospectors. Small test explosions on land (4) and sea (5) send shock, or seismic, waves through the rocks for analysis (6, 7).

11

4

6

The lifeless surface of a Middle Eastern desert gives no hint of the rich energy trapped below.

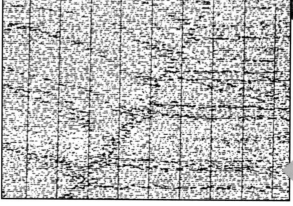

Seismometers record shockwaves altered by passing through rock layers.

IN THE GROUND

Geophysical studies use ground-penetrating radar that reveals changes in rock layers yards (meters) below the surface. Lasers measure rock shift or movement after test explosions.

On land (8) and at sea (9), sensitive devices called gravimeters and magnetometers detect variations in Earth's gravity and magnetism caused by rocks below.

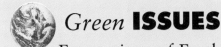

1

2

3

Tiny amounts of gas bubbling from the seabed are sensed by a "sniffer" that checks for various chemicals (10). If all the clues indicate gas or oil below, small drilling rigs dig test wells (11), or an underwater well is dug from an offshore platform (12).

9

7

5

10

12

Geologists check the results from drilled test wells.

BIG RIGS

Tapping oil and natural gas reserves is "boring" work. Wells are drilled — or "bored" — to remove the fuels.

Hundreds of workers live on offshore rigs.

ALL AT SEA

A fixed-leg rig (1) stands on stilt-like legs on the inshore seabed. The greatest water depth for these rigs is about 1,300 feet (400 m).

1

PARTS OF THE RIG

A drilling rig has several parts. Its wide, flat base is called a platform. The tower is known as a derrick. The drill itself is a long series of steel pipes, called a string, tipped with a cutting bit (see page 15). Rig design differs depending on location — on land, inshore, or offshore.

Fierce storms, fires, and shipping accidents may damage rigs. Old rigs are sunk on purpose in deep water (right), if their wells run dry.

A diver checks a rig underwater.

Ocean rigs have two lifelines: helicopters for emergencies and staff transport; and ships for routine supplies, such as food and equipment.

The floating rig (2) has giant buoyancy tanks filled with air or oil. It may be tied by cables to blocks on the seabed, as a "tension-leg" rig.

2

Tension-leg rigs work in water up to 3,300 feet (1,000 m) deep. Farther out (3), anchors, thrusters (propellers in various directions), and satellite navigation keeps the rig ship "on station."

3

The "nodding donkey" is a small production unit that lifts up oil day and night.

Green ISSUES

Ocean rigs are exposed, isolated places, and their work with oil and natural gas involves many hazards. In the North Sea in 1988, the Piper Alpha platform suffered a gas leak and serious fire, and 167 people died — the world's worst rig tragedy. Many safety improvements followed.

Piper Alpha blazes, North Sea

EXPLORE, PRODUCE

Exploratory rigs are the first big arrivals at a possible new inshore or offshore oil or natural gas field. Rigs drill test bores to check the depth and extent of the field. If the field is worth tapping, then production wells are bored. A production platform without a derrick may replace the exploratory rig — which moves to the next site.

DRILLING DEEP

The drill tip — or "bit" — is the cutting edge of the oil and gas industry. Its tip spins and grinds through thousands of feet (meters) of solid rock.

HOW THE DRILL WORKS

The drill "string" consists of lengths of pipe screwed together. Workers add lengths at the upper end as the cutting bit at the lower end bores deeper. In a rotary drill, a diesel engine spins a platform turntable (rotary table) into which the entire "string" of pipes is clamped.

The platform turntable is stopped while a new section (length) of pipe is added to the drill string.

It's a blowout! In many fields, oil is under huge pressure deep in the rocks. It may blast through the taps and valves of a well head.

Green ISSUES

A blowout (above) not only wastes valuable oil, but also pollutes the surroundings. Special equipment is needed to "cap," or control, the flow of oil or fire. Legendary oil man "Red" Adair has capped many blowouts and oil-well fires around the world.

Oil-capper "Red" Adair

Control room

Derrick

Cables

Turntable

Figure 1

Mud pump

In directional drilling (Figure 1), the bit spins as the drill string stays still. Mud, pumped at high pressure down the string pipe, turns a spiral motor near the bit (Figure 2). Mud also cools the bit and carries drilled-off rock back to the surface. The bit is tilted at a slight angle to cut a curve (Figure 3). The production string has holes that allow oil to flow in.

Mud pipe

Blowout valve at well head

Sections of pipe wait their turn to join the drill string.

Information from sensors in the drill string and bit is fed to the control room.

Drill string

Mud flows up around string to surface.

Mud flows down pipe string to bit.

Drill force sensors

Drill direction sensors

Collars prevent string from buckling.

Figure 3

Oil

Gas

Oil out

Well perforations

Water

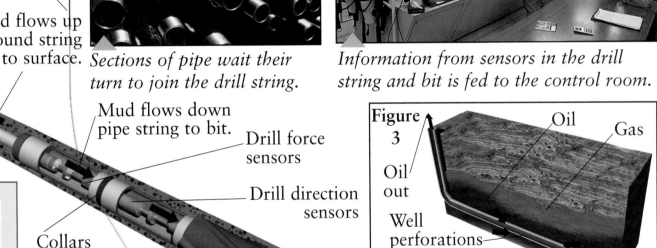

Figure 2 Mud spray cools and flushes rock pieces from spinning bit.

Mud-powered spiral motor

Rock temperature and hardness sensors

Drill bits tipped with diamond dust

RIG TO REFINERY

Oil and natural gas are found in many remote places, from Earth's frozen poles to its steamy tropics. They must be transported to refineries to make into fuels and products.

A supertanker may deliver enough oil in one load to supply a large city with enough fuel to last for more than one year.

OVER THE LAND

About two-thirds of all oil comes from underground. Oil is a liquid that can be forced by powerful pumps along a pipeline laid on the surface or buried below. Booster or relay pumps give an extra push every few dozen miles (kilometers).

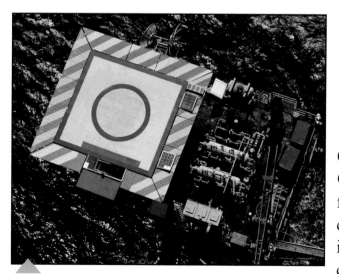

Some production rigs are completely automated. Helicopters visit at intervals to perform routine maintenance.

OVER AND UNDER THE SEA

Mooring buoy
Giant tankers tie up to a floating buoy with its own helipad, waiting to load.

LPG (liquid petroleum gas)
Natural gas is squeezed into a liquid in huge spheres to greatly reduce its volume.

Oil storage
Oil flows from wells continuously. It is stored in massive containers called cells fixed to the seabed, away from wave and storm damage.

ACROSS THE OCEAN

Thick, gooey oil flows very slowly through pipelines, especially in cold places where low temperatures make it thicker. In that case, it's more efficient to pipe it into a supertanker for an ocean journey. Oil and gas from offshore platforms are also loaded into tankers. Inshore platforms near refineries have their own pipelines.

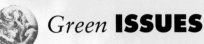

Green **ISSUES**

Oil sometimes spills by accident from a pipe or tanker. At sea, it floats as a thick black slick. This devastates sea life, such as birds and fish, for many years in the future.

Rescuing an oiled guillemot

Refinery
A tanker fills enormous storage cells and sets off again.

Unloading
Oil refineries need plenty of mooring space. Supertankers need 12 miles (20 km) to turn or stop.

North America's longest pipeline crosses 2,400 miles (3,787 km).

Undersea pipeline
A large oil field often has its own pipeline and refinery built nearby. Smaller fields are served by tanker transport.

AT THE OIL REFINERY

Crude oil (petroleum) straight from the ground is not a single substance. It is composed of many hundreds of different substances.

HEATED

A refinery uses heat and pressure to separate crude oil into its many different substances, or constituents. High temperatures change the majority of crude oil's constituents into gases and vapors. These flow along a main pipe into a very tall fractionation tower, or column, (see page 19) which may be more than 328 feet (100 m) tall.

A refinery is a giant maze of pipes, tubes, towers, and tanks that run twenty-four hours a day. Some products from refined oil are reheated for further separation. Others are remixed or blended to make special products, such as kerosene for jet engines.

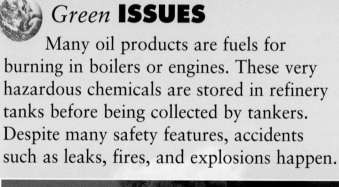

Green ISSUES

Many oil products are fuels for burning in boilers or engines. These very hazardous chemicals are stored in refinery tanks before being collected by tankers. Despite many safety features, accidents such as leaks, fires, and explosions happen.

Monitors check the refining process.

A refinery fire in Hamburg, Germany

COOLED

In a fractionation tower, the separated vapors and gases cool and condense back into liquids. Different levels in the tower stay at various temperatures, which allows collection of the individual substances through a series of pipes.

FRACTIONS OF OIL

The fractionation tower is hot at the bottom and cooler at the top. Products obtained at each level are called fractions. A complex mixture of gases and vapors from heated crude oil enters at the bottom and rises. The thickest, heaviest substances drain off at the base of the tower. Slightly heavier ones condense (turn into liquid) just above, and so on. The lightest gases exit near the top.

86° F (30°C)

Coolest part of tower

Gases for bottled fuels (propane, butane)

Solvents and chemicals for industry

Light fuels (paraffin, kerosene)

Medium fuels (gasoline)

Heavy fuels (diesel, heating oils)

Chemicals

Light lubricating oils

Heavy fuel oils (for ships, heating)

Thick lubricating oils and waxes

Vapors and gases from heated crude oil

752° F (400°C)

Hottest part of tower

Tars, bitumens, pitches, asphalts

19

FUELS FROM OIL

Around the world, about one-third of all the oil pumped out of the ground is used as fuel for cars, trucks, ships, trains, and airplanes.

GAS POWER

Gasoline is the single biggest, most important product made from oil, and the one with which people are most familiar. Although gasoline is a product of refined crude oil, it is not a pure substance. Instead, gasoline is a complex mixture of many substances — chiefly hydrocarbons, which are chemicals made from the elements hydrogen and carbon. When burned, a tank of gasoline releases ten times more heat energy than a coal pile of the same weight.

Filling the gas tank is a regular chore for drivers. Gasoline is not a renewable energy source.

NO OIL, NO GO

Vehicles such as cars need oil — and not just for gasoline. Nearly all the lubricating fluids for the gears and other moving parts are made from crude oil. Hydraulic (pressure) fluids in brakes and suspension cables are also made from oil.

Gas tank
Gearbox oil
Engine oil
Brake hydraulic fluid
Lubricating grease

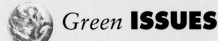 *Green* **ISSUES**

Exhaust fumes from vehicles contain chemicals such as oxides of sulphur. Diesel exhausts also release tiny specks, or particulates. These substances collect in calm, sunny weather over traffic-choked cities and form smog — which causes breathing difficulties and other health problems.

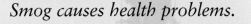

Smog causes health problems.

Diesel fuel is similar to gasoline but usually powers larger engines.

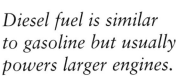

Fuels for special vehicles, such as race cars, are continually improved to release more of their chemical energy as heat, while causing less engine wear.

A cross-country flight aboard a commercial airplane uses fewer gallons per mile than a family car.

21

NATURAL GAS

Natural "gas" is really natural "gases."
Like oil, these formed deep in the ground.
Refineries separate and purify the gases.

GAS USAGE

About about nine-tenths of
the gas in a natural gas field
is methane. This is the
substance also given off by
rotting food and compost
heaps and is sometimes

called "marsh gas." Gases similar to methane
are ethane, propane, butane, and pentane.
These are transported in tankers, cylinders,
or bottles. Most are burned for heating, in
industry and homes, and cooking.

Natural gas varies in its makeup.
When it arrives by pipeline it is
checked for "slugs" — unwanted
gases such as carbon dioxide.
The methane is separated from
the other gases by pressure and
temperature and
piped separately.

*Slug-catcher units
remove pockets of
unwanted gases,
or "slugs,"
before refining.*

2 Slug catcher

1 Natural gas
pipeline

5 Bulk
methane is also
cooled into a
liquid and shipped by
special liquid natural
gas (LNG) tankers.

*A gas refinery
yields fuel for
burning and
raw materials
for industry.*

6 Non-methane
gases flow to
fractionating
columns for
separation.

Non-methane gases pass to tall fractionating towers, where they are heated and cooled as in an oil refinery. The purified gases are collected by ship or truck. Propane is burned for home central heating; butane is popular for camping stoves.

3 Bulk methane is separated from other gases.

Rounded storage tanks resist the great pressure of the gas inside.

4 Bulk methane is delivered for direct burning by pipeline network.

10 Remaining gases used as mixed fuels or by chemical industry.

9 Propane and butane are collected by ship or truck.

8 Propane and butane are pressurized and stored in spherical tanks.

Tanker trucks visit the refinery around the clock. Hazardous loads are identified with warning symbols.

7 Supertankers transport ethane to a chemical plant.

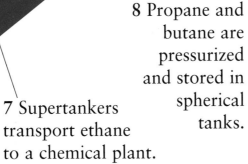

RAW MATERIALS

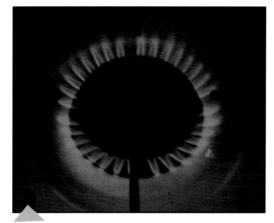

Only about one-hundredth of all natural gas is burned in homes for cooking and heating.

Wherever you are — home or school, at the mall, office, or factory, in a car or train or plane — items made from oil and gas are all around.

PETROCHEMICALS

After oil and natural gas are refined into fuels, many substances remain. They form the basis of the giant petrochemicals industry. Natural gas contains sulphur and nitrogen chemicals that are processed into fertilizers that add valuable nutrients to the soil.

Bags of chemical fertilizers help enrich the soil and maintain high levels of crop production.

Safety ISSUES

Gas is a relatively clean, efficient fuel, but if it leaks and there's a spark nearby — BOOM! Despite many safety precautions, there are several accidental gas explosions in homes, factories, and industrial sites annually.

Result of a gas blast

Towering "cracking" units break apart refined oil chemicals to create simpler substances.

Paints contain solvents, pigments, and fillers — all made from oil.

Some private vehicles run on natural gas, but the type of storage tank needed requires great pressures — and raises safety issues.

"CRACKING" OIL

Substances from the refined oil and gas are further changed by a process called cracking — heating under pressure with various chemicals. The cracking process results in an almost endless list of products — dyes, soaps, shampoos, cleaning fluids, synthetic rubbers, solvents, pesticides, cosmetics …

Natural gas burns fairly "clean," with fewer fumes and particulates compared to gasoline or diesel, making it a good fuel for big cities.

27

POWERING THE WORLD

The main single use of oil and natural gas is to burn in power plants to produce electricity. When burned, oil and natural gas release their energy as heat.

CHANGING FORMS OF ENERGY

A power plant converts energy several times. As the chemical energy locked up in oil or natural gas is burned, it releases massive amounts of heat energy that boils water into high-pressure steam. The steam, in turn, spins huge fan-like turbines, giving them kinetic (moving) energy.

THE POWER PLANT

Oil or natural gas burn to release heat that vaporizes water to steam. As steam spins the angled blades of the turbines (such as the turbine, right), a central shaft also spins. Huge wire coils (the rotor) on the shaft spin in a field of magnetism made by the "stator" around them. Moving wire within a magnetic field produces electricity.

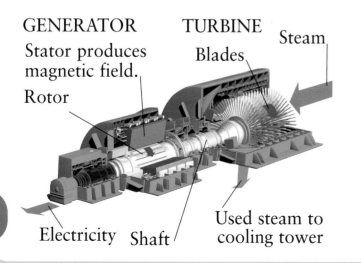

GENERATOR
Stator produces magnetic field.
Rotor

TURBINE
Blades
Steam

Electricity   Shaft

Used steam to cooling tower

Huge stores of natural gas discovered in the 1980s led to a "dash for gas" as gas-fired power plants replaced oil ones.

ELECTRICAL POWER

The last stage in the power plant is where the spinning turbines are linked to a generator. That is where the moving shaft — turning within the powerful magnetism it creates — is converted into electricity.

Around the world, oil-fired power plants produce one-eighth of all electricity. Gas-fired plants make more, about one-sixth, for less overall pollution — but these amounts vary widely. The United States is by far the most oil-thirsty nation in the world, and meets more than one-third of its electric-power needs by burning oil.

Modern gas-fired power plants such as Hitachi's Goldendale HRSG (Heat Recovery Steam Generator) use new "combined cycle" technology. The plant uses natural gas for its main turbines; waste gases turn a second turbine and generator.

 Green **ISSUES**

Most electricity is produced by burning three fossil fuels — coal, oil, and natural gas. Stores of these fossil fuels are running out. When burned, these fuels release many kinds of pollution — as well as greenhouse gases — which may cause global warming.

Electric power versus air pollution

OIL AND GAS FUTURE?

Oil and natural gas are non-renewable fossil fuels. We are using them at a record pace. How long will they last, and how can we extend this time?

Oil may be extracted from shale (see pages 8–9) when supplies run low in the future.

Plant oils can be used as fuels.

WORLD STORES

At present rates of use, our oil and natural gas reserves may run out in sixty and eighty years, repectively. As new deposits are discovered, these estimates may increase. The best plan for our energy future is to develop renewable sources and decrease fossil-fuel use all around.

OIL AND GAS RESERVES

Supporters of oil and gas say there are more reserves now than twenty years ago — thanks to the discovery of new fields.

Such discoveries cannot continue forever. Nations that use the most oil, such as the U.S., can help by burning less.

Oil and its uses are major global issues.

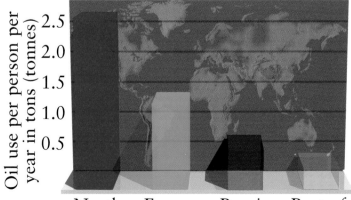

Oil use per person per year in tons (tonnes): 2.5, 2.0, 1.5, 1.0, 0.5

North America   Europe   Russia   Rest of World

GLOSSARY

drill string: a series of drill pipes screwed together with the cutting bit at the end.

geophysical: the physical features of rocks and minerals, such as hardness and color.

inshore: near the shore or coastline, in depths ranging from 164 to 820 feet (50 to 250 m).

laser: short for Light Amplification by Stimulated Emission of Radiation — a very pure form of light energy caused by the natural movement of atoms and molecules jumping from one energy level to another; useful in measuring, cutting, and surgery.

monomers: simple molecules that can link into chains, called polymers.

offshore: in deep water, away from the shore or coastline.

prospecting: searching for mineral resources such as oil, gas, coal, metals, or crystals.

radar: short for RAdio Detecting And Ranging — a system that locates objects and measures speeds and distances using reflected radiowaves.

salt dome: salt minerals that form a "dome" when under high pressure and temperatures; often found near oil and gas fields.

satellite navigation: pinpointing a location using a GPS (global positioning system) receiver that detects satellite signals.

MORE BOOKS TO READ

Exxon Valdez: Oil Spill. Environmental Disasters (series). Nichol Bryan (Gareth Stevens)

Oil Power of the Future: New Ways of Turning Petroleum into Energy. Library of Future Energy (series). Linda Bickerstaff (Rosen)

Oil Rig Workers: Life Drilling for Oil. Extreme Careers (series). Katherine White (Rosen)

What If We Run Out of Fossil Fuels? What If (series). Kimberly M. Miller (Children's Press)

WEB SITES

Discover the underwater aspects of gas and oil exploration and its environmental effects.
www.mms.gov/ommpacific/enviro/ scubadivingteam.htm

Look down an oil well; also contains information and links to natural gas web sites.
www.fe.doe.gov/education/energylesons/oil/ index.html

Due to the dynamic nature of the Internet, some web sites stay current longer than others. To find additional web sites, use a reliable search engine with one or more of the following keywords: *Alaskan pipeline, fossil fuels, gas-fired power plants, natural gas, oil spills, oil rigs, supertankers.*

INDEX